Funny Poems to give you the Giggles

 *weeeee!*

Look out for other books by Susie Gibbs:

Funny Poems to give you the Giggles

Collected by Susie Gibbs
Illustrated by Kelly Waldek

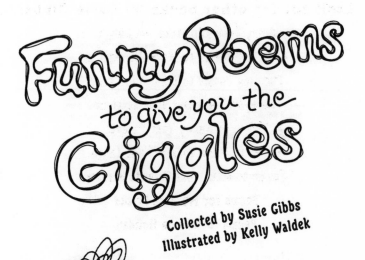

OXFORD
UNIVERSITY PRESS

OXFORD
UNIVERSITY PRESS

Great Clarendon Street, Oxford OX2 6DP

Oxford University Press is a department of the University of Oxford.
It furthers the University's objective of excellence in research, scholarship,
and education by publishing worldwide in

Oxford   New York

Auckland   Cape Town   Dar es Salaam   Hong Kong   Karachi
Kuala Lumpur   Madrid   Melbourne   Mexico City   Nairobi
New Delhi   Shanghai   Taipei   Toronto

With offices in

Argentina   Austria   Brazil   Chile   Czech Republic   France   Greece
Guatemala   Hungary   Italy   Japan   Poland   Portugal   Singapore
South Korea   Switzerland   Thailand   Turkey   Ukraine   Vietnam

Oxford is a registered trade mark of Oxford University Press
in the UK and in certain other countries

British Library Cataloguing in Publication Data
Data available

ISBN-13: 978-0-19-272605-6
ISBN-10: 0-19-272605-6

1 3 5 7 9 10 8 6 4 2

Printed in Great Britain by Cox & Wyman,
Berkshire, Reading

Contents

Clooless

Police station in a panic:
A thief has stolen their loo!
'You mean just the seat?' said the sergeant.
'No, the seat and the toilet bowl too.'
'Do we have any suspects?' he asked.
'No, Sarge, I'm afraid there's no one
And there's just a blank space where the toilet was.
The truth is we've nothing to go on.'

Eric Finney

_Ha-ha!_

Remember . . .

Wipe your bum
Blow your nose
Don't fart
Or pick your toes.
Wash your hands
Wash your hair
Grow your nails
Don't swear.
Please remember
When you're out
Share nicely
Don't shout.

Please, dear, don't let me down . . .

I worry when your father
Goes out on the town!

Catharine Boddy

Animal Rights

Our cat
Won't use the cat-flap
Any more.
He's started to fight
For his Animal Rights
And insists
That he uses the door.

Lindsay MacRae

The Final Straw

I hit my sister.
My dad got mad.

Dad said, 'Get right in your bed. Now.'
So I did. I got right in.
I slit open the mattress
with a sharpened blade
and I slid right in.
It was a tight fit
between those springs.

So Dad said, 'That's destructive.
Stay in your room. And don't you dare come out.'
So I did.
Monday, Tuesday, Wednesday,
Thursday, Friday.
I stayed in my room.
I got lonely. And hungry.

So Dad said, 'Come down here
and eat some food.
Now you eat everything. You hear?'
So I did.
I ate the egg, the chips, and the beans.
The plate, the knife, the fork.
The table.

So Dad said, 'You've gone too far.
You make me sick to death.'
So I picked up the phone.
I called an ambulance.
'Come quickly. My dad's sick . . .
How sick? Sick to death.'
The sound of sirens
soon filled the street.
They carried Dad off on a stretcher.
They had to strap him down
to stop him struggling.

So Dad said, 'That's the final straw!'
(But it wasn't.
There was a spare one
stuck onto a carton of fruit juice
in the fridge.)

Steve Turner

There Was an Old Man of Peru

There was an old man of Peru,
Who dreamt he was eating his shoe.
  He woke in the night
  In a terrible fright,
And found it was perfectly true.

Anon.

A Mouse in Her Room

A mouse in her room woke Miss Dowd.
She was frightened and screamed very loud.
   Then a happy thought hit her—
   To scare off the critter
She sat up in bed and meowed.

Anon.

There Was a Young Lady of Lynn

There was a young lady of Lynn
Who was so uncommonly thin
   That when she essayed
   To drink lemonade,
She slipped through the straw and fell in.

Anon.

A Ride Home?

'What a great show that was!'
Said the flea to his wife
As they came out into the fog.
'It's a rather unpleasant evening now.
Let's not walk home,
Let's take a dog.'

Eric Finney

Wolf and Flea

'I howl on the prairie,' said Wolf to Flea,
'And that's how I lead the pack.'
'I prowl on the hairy,' said Flea to Wolf,
'And that's why I'm here on your back.'

Eric Finney

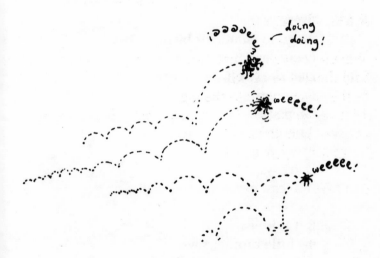

Dad's Birthday Gift

Every year
Gran buys Dad a tie.
Every year
Dad says,
'This is worse than
last year's.
It looks like
her mangy cat's been sick over it.'

Every year
we go to Gran's for birthday tea.
Every year
Dad shows off the new tie.
Every year
Gran says,
'I never know what to buy you.'
Every year
Dad says,
'You can never have enough ties.'

But this year
my little brother says,
'Gran, is your cat feeling better?
Because Dad said it must have been sick on
    his new tie.'

John Coldwell

Jungle Tips

(1) Killer Bee
If you are bitten by a killer bee, bite it right back.
A series of alkaline antibodies will be released which
you may spit on to the wound, neutralizing it. There is
also the keen satisfaction of biting its furry little body
in two.

(2) Piranhas
If you are wading across the Amazon, and a school of
piranhas starts to take an interest, hum like mad whilst
spilling a bottle of tomato ketchup across the river.
They will imagine that you are another bleeding
humming-bird, and will shun you as they cannot
abide feathers stuck to their teeth.

Ivor Cutler

Na-Na-Na-Na!

Ha Ha Ha!

Knock Knock Joke

Knock knock.
Knock knock knock.
Knock knock knock knock knock.

I think they're out.

Adam Smith

Brigadier-General Cornelius Bruff

Brigadier-General Cornelius Bruff
Rode into battle this day in the buff.
A master tactician and incredibly tough
Was Brigadier-General Cornelius Bruff.

The foe that he faced looked on in dismay
As the galloping general came heading their way.
He cried 'Tally-ho!' from the seat of his grey
Just hoping this tactic would win him the day.

His naked assault must have proved quite a sight
For the battle was won, to Bruff's great delight.
It's not that the enemy were frozen with fright;
They were laughing so much that they just couldn't fight.

Richard Caley

Na-Na-Na-Na!

Water Bison

A
water bison
is what
yer wash
yer face in.

Roger McGough

Aitch

'Arry 'Awkins sailed 'is boat
Into ancient Arijaba.
If 'Arry 'ad used 'is aitches
He'd have landed
In Harwich Harbour!

Ha-ha! John Kitching

Ha-Ha!

Snake Riddle

Why didn't the viper
Vipe 'er nose?

Because the adder
'ad 'er 'andkerchief.

Anon.

Have You Read . . . ?

Enjoy Your Homework	by R.U. Joking
Out for the Count	by I.C. Stars
Cliff-Top Rescue	by Justin Time
A Year in Space	by Esau Mars
Your Turn to Wash Up	by Y. Mee
Off to the Dentist	by U. First
Broken Windows	by E. Dunnett
Pickpocket Pete	by M.T. Purse
Lions on the Loose	by Luke Out
Helping Gran	by B.A. Dear
Ten Ice-creams	by Segovia Flaw
Rock Concert	by Q. Here

Judith Nicholls

CLIFF TOP RESCUE — JUSTIN TIME

A YEAR in SPACE by ESAU MARS

YOUR TURN TO WASH UP — Y. MEE

OFF TO THE DENTIST — U. FIRST

BROKEN WINDOWS — E. DUNNETT

PICKPOCKET PETE — M.T. PURSE

LIONS ON THE LOOSE ~ LUKE OUT

Full Bull

A bull,
in a field,
ate a bomb!
Felt ill,
and exceedingly full.
The vet came in haste,
squeezed him all round the waist,
and declared:
  'That's abominable!'

Barry Buckingham

My Newt

I have a newt called Tiny
He's really kind of cute.
The reason he's called Tiny?
Quite simple. He's my newt.

Richard Caley

Another Note from Mom

I sprang from bed and bumped my head and stubbed
  my little toe,
Then jammed my fingers turning down the blaring
  radio.

I rubbed my bumps and bruises as the weather lady
  said,
'Today's the first of April, look for showers overhead.'

I trudged downstairs to breakfast, where my bad luck
  tagged along,
There taped up to the microwave . . . another note
  from Mom:

Good morning! Exclamation point—she always starts
  out nice.
Now comes the part where I get fed her motherly
  advice.

For breakfast, dear, just help yourself. There's pizza in the
  fridge.
And as for soda, choose the Sprite—the Coke has lost its fizz.

'Is this a dream?' I said out loud. 'There must be some
  mistake.
I'd better read that through again. I'm only half awake.'

I scanned the lines, not once, but twice. Yes, *pizza's*
  what it said!
And I could swallow that advice, so I read on ahead:

Please wear your faded jeans to school, those low-cut ones
  that flare.
And use my mousse to do that sticky-up thing with your hair.

'Is she for real?' I asked myself. What's gotten into Mom?
Whatever it was, I liked it lots, so I continued on:

About your science quiz today—the one on natural gas—
Just tell your teacher that's one subject you don't want to pass!

I know I didn't read that right, I couldn't have, no way!
But there it was in black and white, as plain as night
  and day.

And then it hit me, why the change: Mom hadn't lost
  a screw;
My worry-free philosophy had finally gotten through.

Her rules had changed from lame to lax—my mom was
  cool at last!
These last few months of middle school were gonna be
  a blast!

I quickly read the last few lines: Enjoy your day at school!
(And don't believe what you've just read ... or you're an April
  Fool!)

Diane Z. Shore

A Date with Fate

(written on the tombstone of a girl who died on June 1st)

Dear May lies here—
she lived in fear
of perishing
this very day.

I guess she knew
the first of June
would prove to be
the end of May!

Graham Denton

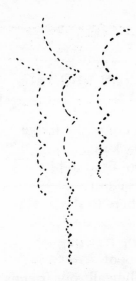

A Lesson Learned

One day my skydiving Uncle Newt
forgot to pack his parachute.
'That's one mistake,' said Auntie Jen,
'that he will never make again.'

Bruce Lansky

The Rival Arrives

Tom, take the baby out of the fridge
And put the milk back in.
We know you are not used to him
And think he makes a din,
But I'm afraid he's here to stay
And he is rather cute,
So you'll have to stop insisting
He goes in the car-boot.
And please stop telling all your friends
We bought him in a sale,
Or that he's a free sample
We received in the mail.
He was *not* found in a trolley
At the local Mothercare,
And a family did not give him to us
Because they'd one to spare.

You should look on the bright side, Tom.
In just a year or two
You will have someone else to blame
For the wicked things you do.

Brian Patten

There Was an Old Man of Blackheath

There was an old man of Blackheath
Who sat on his set of false teeth.
  Said he with a start,
   'Oh, Lord, bless my heart!
I have bitten myself underneath!'

Anon.

True Love

'Your teeth are like the stars,' he said,
And pressed her hand so white.
He spoke the truth, for, like the stars,
Her teeth came out at night.

Anon.

About the Teeth of Sharks

The thing about a shark is—teeth,
One row above, one row beneath.

Now take a close look. Do you find
It has another row behind?

Still closer—here, I'll hold your hat:
Has it a third row behind that?

Now look in and . . . Look out! Oh my,
I'll *never* know now! Well, goodbye.

John Ciardi

Chicken School Timetable

Period one—simple clucking
Period two—more clucking
Period three—clucking with attitude
Period four—clucking with indecision
Period five—pecking in dirt
Period six—pecking in gravel
Period seven—rhythmic and jerky neck movements
Period eight—clucking (revision)

Roger Stevens

Lonely Heart

Handsome, lean wolf
Likes acting and cooking
Tired of old grannies
Is currently looking
For lady in red
With plump and soft skin
To share walks in the forest
And cosy nights in.

Rachel Rooney

There Was a Young Man of Japan

There was a young man of Japan
Whose limericks never would scan;
   When they said it was so,
   He replied, 'Yes, I know,
But I always try to get as many words into the last
   line as ever I possibly can.'

Anon.

There Was a Young Man of St Bees

There was a young man of St Bees
Who was stung on the arm by a wasp;
   When they said, 'Does it hurt?'
   He replied, 'No it doesn't.
It's a good job it wasn't a hornet.'

Anon.

Na Na Na Na Na!

The Orang-utan

The closest relative of man
They say, is the orang-utan;
And when I look at Grandpapa,
I realize how right they are.

Colin West

Ha Ha!

Bald Patch

Grandad isn't going bald,
that's just the way it grows;
his hair's not falling off his head,
it's escaping out his nose.

Rachel Rooney

Little Dog

Ahh . . . little dog
Ah . . . you look all lonely and lost
You lickle diddums

Are you following me now?

Oh . . . you are a friendly one,
    aren't you, doggy?
Ooh—you're tickling my leg!
Ooh—don't!

Ooh—that hurts
Hey come on—
don't chew my ankle!

Could you get off, please?

Just . . . just . . . just . . . OW!

I'm getting VERY ANGRY NOW

Oi ! ! ! ! !

THAT REALLY HURTS

NOW HOP IT

YOU HORRIBLE
UGLY
MONSTER

James Carter

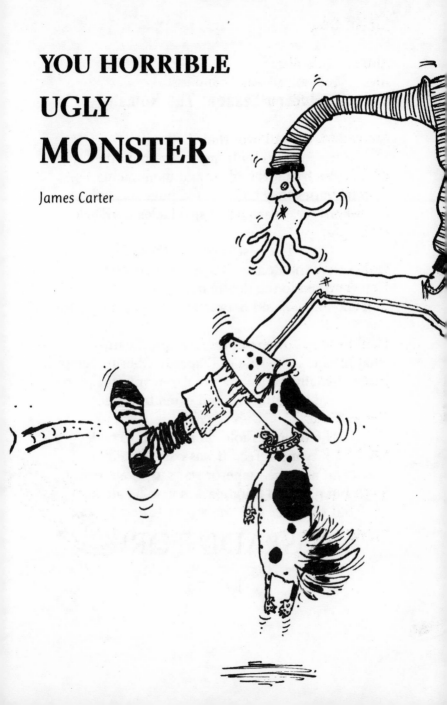

History Lesson: The Romans

All over their Empire
the Romans built impressive buildings
such as forts, villas, and monuments.
In big cities they constructed huge *Amphitheatres*
where great games and spectacles were held.

The best known of these
are the Roman Games with contests,
often to the death, between animals,
between men and between women combatants.

It was in one of these amphitheatres
that Miranda, the wife of Emperor Tiberius Tempus,
accidentally fell from her balcony into the arena
and was attacked and eaten by a tiger.

The tiger was told off and sent to bed.
Everyone agreed it was bad he ate her,
and now the Emperor was sad he ate her,
and poor old Miranda was mad he ate her,
but the tiger said she was tasty and he was

GLADIATOR!

John Rice

Bird-Watching

The book said,
'Look for birds with binoculars.'

So I looked, but I couldn't find any.
I found plenty who had their own telescopes though.

Melissa Lawrence

Shame

A wicked old lady headteacher
was attacked by a man-eating creature,
  though hardly dismayed,
  pupils went to her aid
but slightly too slowly to reach her.

Trevor Parsons

No Room to Swing a Cat!

My hotel room was tiny.
No room to swing a cat.
My cat was overjoyed and said,
'Well, thank the Lord for that!'

Colin McNaughton

Elephant Embarrassment

Alone among the bathing beasts
The elephants face ridicule:
They just can't keep their trunks up
So they won't go in the pool.

Eric Finney

In For a Shock

A tadpole swam to the side of his pond
Where a frog was having a doze.
  'What a horrible creature,'
  The tadpole cried.
'I'm glad I'm not one of those.'

Cynthia Rider

Upgrading Granny

Granny's been to the hospital
She needed an upgrade again
Her body's been stripped and refitted
By an army of white-coated men

Her new teeth are pure carbon fibre
Her specs were designed with a laser
She can now bite through plates if she wants to
And her eyesight's as sharp as a razor

She's got digital hearing aid power
And her pacemaker's nuclear I'm told
They replaced her hip with a stainless steel joint
And her Zimmer's now radio-controlled

There was a special offer on memory
She got 64 megs of it free
She can now recall where she left Grandad
And that I owe her 35p

Her toilet's controlled by computer
Her electric shopping cart's fun
Her stairlift's got internet access
I can't wait till I'm ninety-one

Andy Seed

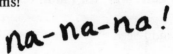

Ark Anglers

Noah let his sons go fishing,
Only on the strictest terms:
'Sit still; keep quiet and concentrate:
We've only got two worms!'

Celia Warren

Cake Mistake

Mother made a birthday cake,
For icing she used glue.
The children sit so quiet now,
Andchewandchewandchew.

Douglas Florian

Squelch!

I am a dainty Brontosaurus,
  Skipping through the meadow.
Oops-a-daisy! Pardon me!
  Must watch where I tread-o!

(Silly place to have a picnic anyway!)

Colin McNaughton

Cannibal Tips

Never lend a hand to a cannibal,
even if he looks a bit distressed.
No, never give a hand to a cannibal,
the chances are he'll only want the rest.

And don't lose your heart to a cannibal,
or let him catch your eye or pick your brain.
Nor, just for fun, should you let one pull your leg;
if it stays attached he'll try again.

Avoid playing foot ball with cannibals,
it could be one of yours and come to harm.
In short, keep a cannibal at arm's length
and, preferably, use someone else's arm.

Trevor Parsons

Na-Na-Na!

A Platter's Not a Laughing Matter

A cannibal, Clarence McDunny,
Made a stew not of lamb, fish, or bunny,
    But of cooked circus clown
    Which he couldn't get down,
For he thought: Gosh, this meal sure tastes *funny*!

Robert Scotellaro

Ha-ha!

A Sleeper from the Amazon

A sleeper from the Amazon
Put nighties of his gra'mazon.
    The reason, that
    He was too fat
To get his own pyjamazon.

Anon.

Shaking

Geraldine now, stop shaking that cow
For heaven's sake, for your sake and the cow's sake.
That's the dumbest way I've seen
To make a milk shake.

Shel Silverstein

Moon Landing Fails!

'Unable to land on Moon,' came the message.
'Returning to Earth quite soon.'
'Why unable to land?' Earth radioed back.
The reply was, 'It's a full moon.'

Eric Finney

Polly!

Polly put the kettle on,
Polly put the kettle on,
Polly put the kettle on,

—I HEARD YOU THE FIRST TIME!

Marcus Parry

There Was a Young Lady Whose Nose

There was a Young Lady, whose Nose
Continually prospers and grows;
   When it grew out of sight,
   She exclaimed in a fright,
'Oh! Farewell to the end of my Nose!'

Edward Lear

www

'How dare you call it a web!' said the spider
In a tone very far from polite.
'We spiders are into computing:
It's now called a *website*.'

Eric Finney

Last Request

Major Alexander Phinn
An ancestor of mine,
Was captured by the enemy
Across the River Rhine.
The captain of the firing squad
Asked, 'Is there a last request?'
My Uncle Alex smiled and said,
'Yes please—a bulletproof vest!'

Gervase Phinn

To Be Answered in Our Next Issue

When a great tree falls
And people aren't near,
Does it make a noise
If no one can hear?
And which came first,
The hen or the egg?
This impractical question
We ask and then beg.
Some wise men say
It's beyond their ken.
Did anyone ever
Ask the hen?

Anon.

tueet!

Acknowledgments

Every effort has been made to trace and contact copyright holders before publication and we are grateful to all those who have granted us permission. We apologize for any inadvertent errors and will be pleased to rectify these at the earliest opportunity.

Catherine Boddy: 'Remember' copyright © Catherine Boddy.
Barry Buckingham: 'Full Bull' copyright © Barry Buckingham.
Richard Caley: 'My Newt' and 'Brigadier-General Cornelius Bruff' copyright © Richard Caley.
James Carter: 'Little Dog' copyright © 2002 James Carter from *Cars Stars Electric Guitars* by James Carter. Reproduced by permission of Walker Books Ltd, London SE11 5HJ.
John Ciardi: 'About the Teeth of Sharks' copyright © 1962 by John Ciardi. Used by permission of HarperCollins Publishers.
John Coldwell: 'Dad's Birthday Gift' copyright © John Coldwell.
Graham Denton: 'A Date with Fate' copyright © Graham Denton.
Eric Finney: 'Clooless', 'A Ride Home?', 'Wolf and Flea', 'Elephant Embarrassment', 'Moon Landing Fails!', and 'www' copyright © Eric Finney.
Douglas Florian: 'Cake Mistake' from *Bing Bang Boing*, copyright © 1994 by Douglas Florian, reprinted by permission of Harcourt, Inc.
John Kitching: 'Aitch' copyright © John Kitching.
Bruce Lansky: 'A Lesson Learned' copyright © 2002 by Bruce Lansky. Reprinted from *Funny Little Poems for Funny Little People* (© 2002 by Meadowbrook Creations) with permission from Meadowbrook Press.
Melissa Lawrence: 'Bird-Watching' copyright © Melissa Lawrence.
Lindsay MacRae: 'Animal Rights' from *You Canny Shove Yer Granny Off a Bus!* by Lindsay MacRae (Viking 1995). Copyright © Lindsay MacRae, 1995. Reproduced by permission of Penguin Books Ltd.
Roger McGough: 'Water Bison' by Roger McGough (copyright © Roger McGough 1988) is reproduced by permission of PFD (www.pfd.co.uk) on behalf of Roger McGough.
Colin McNaughton: 'No Room to Swing a Cat!' copyright © 1999 Colin McNaughton from *Wish You Were Here (And I Wasn't)* by Colin McNaughton. 'Squelch!' copyright © 1993 Colin McNaughton from *Making Friends with Frankenstein* by Colin McNaughton. Reproduced by permission of Walker Books Ltd, London SE11 5HJ.
Judith Nicholls: 'Have You Read . . . ?' copyright © Judith Nicholls 2005, from *Shadow Rap* by Judith Nicholls, published by Hodder Murray. Reprinted by permission of the author.
Marcus Parry: 'Polly!' copyright © Marcus Parry.
Trevor Parsons: 'Shame' and 'Cannibal Tips' copyright © Trevor Parsons.